P9-CNA-939

Traumkraut

Yvan Goll's

Dreamweed
Traumkraut

translated by Nan Watkins

Black Lawrence Press

Pittsburgh, PA

Black Lawrence Press
www.blacklawrence.com

Executive Editor: Diane Goettel
Interior Design: Rebecca Maslen
Cover art: "Joe-Pye Weed" by Robert Johnson
Translator photo: Thomas Rain Crowe

The photograph of Yvan Goll is used with permission of the Fondation
Yvan et Claire Goll, Saint-Diè des Vosges, France.

Yvan Goll: Traumkraut. Gedichte aus dem Nachlass.
© Limes Verlag, Wiesbaden, 1951.
Alle Rechte bei und vorbehalten durch Wallstein Verlag, Göttingen.

ISBN: 978-0-9837945-1-6

All rights reserved. Except for brief quotations in critical articles or
reviews, no part of this book may be reproduced in any manner with-
out prior written permission from the publisher:

Black Lawrence Press
326 Bigham Street
Pittsburgh, PA 15211
U.S.A.

Published 2012 by Black Lawrence Press, an imprint of Dzanc Books
Printed in the United States

for Peter

Inhalt

Contents

Introduction

In the poems of his late work, *Dreamweed* (*Traumkraut*), Yvan Goll expresses his keenest suffering, endured and transformed through the power of love. Having avoided the ranks of the German Reich Army during The Great War by relocating in Switzerland, having written in French when his German verse was banned by the rising German Fascists, having taken a late ship from France to his Second World War exile in New York, Yvan Goll, in July 1945, set his sights upon returning to his home in Paris, only to have his lingering illness diagnosed as incurable leukemia. A month later, documents came through declaring him an American citizen.

Upon his return to Europe in 1947, Goll lay in the hospital of the University of Strasbourg—where he had once been a student—and began to record his visions of the mythic flower "alasam," the dreamweed that was to haunt him and beckon him to his death some two years later. In those early days of his illness, Yvan Goll began writing vivid descriptions of his own pain, a pain that he had long perceived in the body politic of the European civilization he inhabited, but that now coursed through his own blood and flesh: "This holy body! / Sacrificial animals roar deep within me / And beef loins exhale their stench every Saturday." His sleepless midnights produced hallucinatory imagery of "The death-drunken trees of my years."

When reading Goll's lyrics, one imagines that he should have inhabited a stellar role within the artistic firmament of early twentieth-century Europe. His talent, his curiosity, and his need to survive the grave upheavals of his time drove him to produce a large creative oeuvre of poetry, drama, fiction, translation, and essays. He moved easily among the French, German, and later the American cultures, describing himself as having "a French heart, a German spirit, a Jewish blood, and an American passport." Yet perhaps his very ability to join in the discussion with so many diverse groups was a limitation in a world moving increasingly toward specialization. No one group has claimed him exclusively, and as a result of such rigid compartmentalization much of his work has slipped into obscurity. A selection of Goll's work is readily available today to the French- and German-reading public, yet he is almost unknown to English-speaking audiences.

Yvan Goll began life on 29 March 1891, as Isaac Lang, in the town of Saint-Dié des Vosges in the contested border region of Alsace-Lorraine. From his earliest days this national rivalry fostered his expression in both French and German. Upon the death of his father, he moved with his French-speaking mother, who called her son Mignon, to the provincial capital of Metz, where he attended the local German Lyceum. His university studies took him to Strasbourg, Freiburg, and Munich, until in 1914, with the outbreak of The Great War, Goll moved to Switzerland. There he studied at Lausanne and connected with the Dadaists in Zurich (German) and the pacifist circles in both Zurich and Geneva (French). Some of his earliest poems were anti-war laments, including his collection, *Requiem für die Gefallenen von Europa*. During the tumultuous war years, the young Isaac Lang began signing his publications with various pseudonyms until he settled upon the name Yvan Goll. It was during his time in Switzerland that he met the gifted poet, Claire Studer, just before she would show her work to Rainer Maria Rilke. The mutual attraction between Yvan and Claire was immediate, and the two became life partners; in 1919 they moved to Paris and married there in 1921.

Goll's natural place in the avant-garde took him to Berlin, where he found Expressionism to be an outlet for his post-war thinking. The premier performance of his satirical play, *Methusalem, oder der ewige Bürger*, with set design by George Grosz, took place in the Dramatic Theater of Berlin and was a precursor to Ionesco and the Theatre of the Absurd. Returning to Paris, he became immersed in Surrealism, first championing Apollinaire, then opposing Breton in his own Surrealist Manifesto, published simultaneously with Breton's first Manifesto in October 1924. Goll wrote essays on film and theater and Cubism; he translated Walt Whitman, Franz Werfel, Stefan Zweig and Emil Ludwig; he published in French and German journals and worked with the

Rhein Verlag in Switzerland to publish the new work of other writers, including James Joyce, whose *Ulysses* was being translated into German by Georg Goyert. He joined Samuel Beckett and a few others to translate a section of Joyce's *Finnegans Wake* into French. In his own publishing efforts he enlisted artists of the first rank, including Chagall, Dali, Grosz, Tanguy, Delaunay, Léger, and Picasso to illustrate his books and journals. During the 1920s his many novels, including *Sodome et Berlin,* decried the lack of order in the modern world.

In 1931 Goll met the Austrian poet and painter Paula Ludwig, who was to become his second muse. The 1930s, then, became an increasingly tense time, not only on the world stage, but also in Goll's personal and professional life. In 1933 his work was blacklisted by the German government, making it impossible for him to be published in German. His solution was to translate his works into French so that they could be published in France. In 1935 he attended the first large Author Congress in Paris to protest the rising tide of Fascism. Troubled by the state of the world, in 1936 Goll began to write a series of poems using a modern Everyman character, Jean sans Terre (Landless John), to depict the homeless, wandering Jew. He continued to add poems to *Jean Sans Terre* throughout the rest of his life. After his death, a group of American poets, including W.S. Merwin, Kenneth Rexroth, Galway Kinnell, William Carlos Williams, Kenneth Patchen, and Louise Bogen translated a selection of these poems, which appeared in English in 1958.

Goll's allegiance to his wife Claire and his confidante Paula, both of whom were living in Paris under the threat of the German invasion, finally produced a tension so great that Yvan and Claire left Paris and entered a life of exile in late August 1939. On the 6th of September they arrived in New York where they made their home until 1947.

The Golls settled in a townhouse in Brooklyn Heights, overlooking the East River. According to Miriam Patchen, widow of poet Kenneth Patchen and friend of the Golls, Yvan Goll was at the center of the artistic community in Greenwich Village; their home at 134 Columbia Heights was a gathering place for poets and writers. It is heartening to see how a man with a keen European sensibility immersed himself in the uniqueness of American life, delving into the culture of the Native Americans who had once lived on the spot where he was living. Goll wrote poems in French called "Mannahatta" and "Balcons suspendus sur Lackawanna," all of which were collected into a volume called *Élégie de Lackawanna* and later movingly translated as *Lackawanna Elegy* by Galway Kinnell. Goll was active in the French-American community of New York, where his friends Marc and Bella Chagall were also in exile. He founded his journal *Hemispheres,* where he published his old rival André Breton, Saint-John Perse, William Carlos Williams, Kenneth Patchen, Henry Miller, the young Philip Lamantia, et al. He wrote his "Elegy for James Joyce" for *The Nation.* At the end of the Second World War, Goll wrote, in English, a powerful collection of verse that appeared as *Fruit From Saturn*; it opens with an apocalyptic poem defining the atomic age, "Atom Elegy," which he dedicated to the young American composer and conductor Lukas Foss. "Thus the promethean spark returns / To its dismantled fount..." In his constant search for meaning he explored the worlds of alchemy and mysticism, the symbolism of the Kabbalah and tarot.

When not in New York, the Golls spent summers at the writers' retreats at Yaddo and the MacDowell Colony. Early in their American exile they visited Cuba, yielding Yvan's essay, "Cuba, corbeille de fruits," and poem, "Vénus Cubaine." Later they traveled to the Gaspé Peninsula in Quebec Province, Canada, where Goll was struck by the power of a pierced rock, which he honored in *Le Mythe de la Roche Percée.*

Among the masterpieces in Yvan Goll's large oeuvre are his volumes of love poetry. It was the two women in his life who received his full expression of love in a world torn asunder by the devastation of war. Already in the 1920s, he and Claire had begun to write lyrics to each other, love lyrics that celebrated their life together. Early volumes carried the titles *Poèmes d'amour, Poèmes de jalousie, Poèmes de la vie et de la mort.* In Goll's extensive correspondence with Paula Ludwig, he included love poems written in

German, which were later collected as *Malaüsche Liebeslieder*. The volume that spans the arc of Yvan and Claire's 30 years together is *10,000 Dawns*, originally published in both French and German and translated into English by Thomas Rain Crowe and Nan Watkins. The title poem was written by Yvan to celebrate the thirtieth anniversary of the day they met. On 10 February 1947, Yvan slipped the poem under Claire's door in New York, celebrating their life together: "10,000 dawns, my angel, 10,000 dawns."

After seeking medical help in New York for his leukemia, in 1947 Yvan Goll decided to return to France. His mind became haunted by a "dreamweed," and he began conceiving poems in German. Within a year, he submitted five poems for publication, with the explanation to the editor: "After a twenty-year departure, I have returned to the German language with devotion and desire for renewal, and a throbbing heart. Surrealism has passed through me and deposited its salt. Yet for me it is as though this dreamweed plant is a new birth. I have returned late to Europe and find many gates black and in ruins...." The poems were accepted for publication, and Yvan continued to write, whether he was in a hospital bed, or in his apartment in Paris, or traveling to read his work. Some poems described his pain, his anguish at being ensnared by disease, thus having to face death. Others were love poems to Claire as she stayed by him in his final months, weeks, and days. In the Fall of 1949, Yvan traveled to the PEN Club meeting in Venice, and on the way home he stopped in Zurich to record a reading at Radio Beromünster. He introduced his poems by saying, "Now I will read the poems from my last, still unpublished volume, *Das Traumkraut.*"

Throughout Goll's life, he worked tirelessly to promote the work of other poets, so it was not unusual that in his last months he would welcome into his home the young Rumanian poet who had recently moved to Paris, known as Paul Celan. The two rapidly developed a rapport, Celan offering to translate some of Goll's poems and Goll asking Celan to be one of his literary executors. Not long after their meeting, Goll entered the Hôpital Americaine in Neuilly, near Paris, on 13 December 1949, never to return home.

In the last weeks of his life, Yvan Goll was consumed with completing his poems inspired by "das Traumkraut" or the dreamweed. The poems appeared on every scrap of paper he could find--envelopes, prescriptions, newspaper margins--all written "with the tiny birds of his beautiful handwriting." Poets of many nationalities, including the young Paul Celan, lined up to donate blood so that Yvan could finish his work. But after great suffering and a prolonged battle for his life, Yvan Goll succumbed to death on 27 February 1950. His body was finally laid to rest in the Père Lachaise Cemetery in Paris, opposite the grave of Chopin.

In these *Dreamweed* poems, death becomes Yvan Goll's familiar, and love is his salvation in a winter world of pain. The snow creates a death mask for him. His body is no longer his body but a hostel for his ancestors' bones; his heart is plundered for iron; his kidneys are meat for a bloodhound; his flesh is consumed by eternal fire. Yet wandering down the road to death and tumbling down the steps into the ocean of time, Yvan Goll, in the guise of Jean sans Terre, continues to seek and question. Ultimately it is love that sustains him as his earthly body crumbles to dust and his spirit rises from the confines of his hospital bed to soar freely among the stars in the vastness of eternal night.

April 2012
Nan Watkins
Tuckasegee, North Carolina

Sprengung der Dotterblume

Gewittergelb

Wie Blick von Amazonen

Voll Lüsternheit des Chroms

Entsteigt die schwangere Dotterblume

Dem Ahnenteich

Sprengt

Der Götter Einsamkeit

Der Lerchen Lachen macht mich schaudern

Explosion of the Marsh Marigold

Storm yellow

Like the leer of Amazons

Filled with the lust of chrome

The pregnant marsh marigold rises

From the ancestral pond

Exploding

The solitude of the gods

The laughter of the larks makes me shudder

Bluthund

Bluthund vor meinem Herzen

Wachend über mein Feuer

Der du dich nährst von bitteren Nieren

In der Vorstadt meines Elends

Leck mit der nassen Flamme deiner Zunge

Das Salz meines Schweißes

Den Zucker meines Todes

Bluthund in meinem Fleisch

Fang die Träume die mir entfliegen

Bell die weißen Geister an

Bring zurück zu ihrem Pferch

Alle meine Gazellen

Und zerbeiß die Knöchel meines flüchtigen Engels

Bloodhound

Bloodhound at my heart

Who guards my fire

Who feeds on bitter kidneys

In the suburb of my misery

With the wet flame of your tongue

Lick the salt of my sweat

The sugar of my death

Bloodhound in my flesh

Retrieve the dreams that flee from me

Bark at the white ghosts

Bring all my gazelles

Back to their fold

And bite the ankles of my runaway angel

Salz und Phosphor

Entkümmerte sich nur das Salz

In meinem Aug!

Wer wird das Eisen bergen

Aus meinem Herzbergwerk?

Alle meine Metalle

Zersetzen sich in der Erinnerung

Der reine Phosphor tobt sich aus

In meinem Gemüt

Vom schwingenden Achat an meinem Finger

Erwarte ich die Hilfe der Gestirne

Salt and Phosphorus

If only the salt in my eye

Stopped caring!

Who will salvage the iron

In the mine of my heart?

All my metals

Disintegrate in memory

Pure phosphorus rages

In my mind

From the agate brandished on my finger

I await the help of the stars

Irrsal

In den Gärten von Gips

In Morästen von Brom

Wandern die Sterbenden auf elenden Stelzen

Und schwanken Gebeinen

Feuer wedelt noch im südöstlichen Kopf

Eine adlige Blume friert

Im berstenden Brustkorb

Wer hört die Vögel in den Schläfen?

Den Eidechs in den müden Füßen?

Die eilig Lebenden und langsam Sterbenden

Wie sie noch klettern

Am Seile unwirklichen Schlafs!

Nun kommt der Winter dieser hohen Nacht

Der weiße Aether windet die Krone

Um ihr zitterndes Haar

Maze

In gardens of plaster

In swamplands of bromine

The dying wander on rickety stilts

And tottering bones

Flames still flicker in the southeastern skull

A noble flower freezes

In the bursting ribcage

Who can hear the birds in their temples?

The lizard in their tired feet?

Those rushing through life and those slowly dying

How they keep climbing

The rope of unreal sleep!

Now comes the winter of this sublime night

White ether braids the crown

Around its trembling hair

Greise

Euer nelkenfarbenes Fleisch

Das noch von mageren Vögeln zehrt

Und daran Feuer fängt

Singet langsamer ihr Greise

In dem verwandelten Wind

Und laßt die Sonne bröckeln

Zwischen den Fingern

Der blaugefiederte Schlaf

Hat Totenzähne

Und die Stimme des Kalks

Old Men

Your carnation-white flesh

Lives off scrawny birds

And thereby catches fire

You old men, sing slower

In the shifting wind

And let the sun crumble

Between your fingers

Blue-feathered sleep

Has the teeth of death

And the voice of lime

Alasam

Alasam

Die ungeweinte Träne

In der Mulde meines Schädels

Ein Traumkraut wuchs

Nachtgelb mordfahl

Lange lange Menschenalter

Später daraus empor

Einmalige Blume

Unvermerkt von den Bienen

Alasam

Alasam

The unshed tear

In the hollow of my skull

From this there grew

Long long generations later

A dreamweed

Night-yellow murder-sallow

Unique flower

Unnoticed by the bees

Straße durchs Land

Straße durchs Land

Besät mit Jaspis und mit Diamant

Straße der Armen

Lasso um den Nacken der Besessenen

Woher wohin

Im weißen Turban deines Staubs

Wohin woher

Mein Schatten stürzest du?

Country Road

Road through the country

Strewn with jasper and diamonds

Road of the poor

Lasso around the neck of the possessed

From where to where

In the white turban of your dust

To where from where

My shadow do you rush?

Die Kastanienhand

Die Kastanienhand ergriff meine erschrockene Hand

Eine Achtfingerhand voll grüner Schwielen

Und offen jeder Vogelangst

Vor sieben Tagen kaum gebildet noch

Und meine Fünfzigerhand weiß und weich

Ja eine Fleischhand welche viel gemordet und gewürgt

Keimendes Lächeln oder Heckenrosen

Was wollte plötzlich diese Richterhand von ihr?

Und meine Menschenhand erstarrte

Fiel von mir ab

The Chestnut Hand

The chestnut hand grasped my frightened hand

An eight-fingered hand full of green calluses

It was barely formed seven days ago

And exposed to every bird's fear

My fifty-year-old hand soft and white

Yes, a flesh hand that had murdered and strangled

A nascent smile or sundry dog roses

What did this judge's hand suddenly want from mine?

My human hand froze

And fell off

Die inneren Bäume

Die trunkenen

Die todestrunkenen Bäume meiner Jahre

Heiß wachsen sie aus meinem Haupt

Mit Frucht und Wurzel

Mit Händen und mit Sonnen

Behenden und besonnenen Tieren

Im Aug des goldenen Froschs glüht

Das Licht des Saturn

Während auf den Wiesen

Die Kometen blühen

The Inner Trees

The drunken

The death-drunken trees of my years

Grow out of my head

Hot with fruit and root

With hands and with suns

Nimble discreet animals

The light of Saturn glows

In the eye of the golden frog

While on the meadows

The comets bloom

Stunden

Wasserträgerinnen

Hochgeschürzte Töchter

Schreiten schwer herab die Totenstraße

Auf den Köpfen wiegend

Einen Krug voll Zeit

Eine Ernte ungepflückter Tropfen

Die schon reifen auf dem Weg hinab

Wasserfälle Flüsse Tränen Nebel Dampf

Immer geheimere Tropfen immer kargere Zeit

Schattenträgerinnen

Schon vergangen schon verhangen

Ewigkeit

Hours

Water bearers

High-aproned daughters

Walk wearily down the road to death

Each cradling on her head

A tankard of time

A harvest of unpicked drops

That ripen on the way down

Waterfalls rivers tears fog steam

Always more mysterious drops and always less time

Shadow bearers

Already vanished already veiled

In eternity

Der heilige Leib

Behausung meiner Ahnen

Dies schwanke Knochenhaus

Auf Sand gebaut

Aus meinen Augen blicken

Sie allen meinen Straßen nach

Und meine Milz ist ihre Garküche

In der sie kochen mit Fett und Blut

In der Ruinennische schläft noch meine Mutter

Am Kehlkopf klebt der Tabakrauch der Greise

Mein heiliger Leib!

Die Opferstiere brüllen tief in mir

Und Rinderlenden duften samstäglich

Mein Mund beherbergt noch

Jahrhundertalte Magie

In meinen Ohren ist ein Lauschen und ein Rauschen

Und kein Gott

This Holy Body

This shaky house of bones

Built upon sand

Lodging for my ancestors

From my eyes they follow

All the roads I take

My spleen is their kitchen

Where they cook with fat and blood

In the niche of the ruins my mother still sleeps

Old men's tobacco smoke clings to her larynx

My holy body!

Sacrificial animals roar deep within me

And beef loins exhale their stench every Saturday

My mouth still houses

Century-old magic

In my ears I hear a ringing and a singing

And no God

Feuerharfe

Brennender Dornbusch

Anbruch innerster Verwandlung

Feuerharfe

Meiner frühen Schmerzen

Gewicht aus Rauch meines Wunschs

Magre Gluten der Revolten

Rosenbrände meiner Dome

Feuerfester Engel dieser Erde

Aschenrabe

Friß die Reste des Vergessens

Vater aller wilden Flammen

Segne deinen Feuersohn

Fire Harp

Burning brier

Genesis of innermost change

Fire harp

Of my untimely pain

Smoky weight of my desire

Meager embers of revolts

Rose blights of my cathedrals

Fireproof angel of this earth

Cinder raven

Devour the dregs of forgetting

Father of all wild flames

Bless your son of fire

Die Hochöfen des Schmerzes

In den Hochöfen des Schmerzes

Welches Erz wird da geschmolzen

Die Eiterknechte

Die Fieberschwestern

Wissen es nicht

Tagschicht

Nachtschicht allen Fleisches

Blühn die Wunden und die Feuer

Wild in den Salpetergärten

Und den heißen Rosenäckern

Asphodelen meiner Angst

An den Abhängen der Nacht

Ach was braut der Herr der Erze

In den Herzen? Den Schrei

Den Menschenschrei aus dunklem Leib

Der wie ein geweihter Dolch

Unsre Totensonne schlitzt

The Blast Furnaces of Pain

In the blast furnaces of pain

What ore is smelted there?

The servants of pus

The nurses of fever

They have no answer

Day-shift

Night-shift of all flesh

The wounds and the fires

Bloom wild in gardens of saltpeter

And burning fields of roses

Asphodels of my fear

On the cliffs of night

What does the Lord of Ores brew

In our hearts? The cry

The human cry from a dark body

That like a consecrated dagger

Slashes the sun of our dead

Morgue

Im Eis des Schlafs

Wurzelbefreit

Wandert der Träumende

Wandert um nimmer

Wiederzukehren

Zum Gasthaus der Erde

Doch im Abgrund seines Fleisches

Ein altes Feuer baumgeboren

Reift ruhig weiter

Morgue

In the ice of sleep

Unrootbound

The dreamer wanders

Wanders never

Again to return

To the guesthouse of earth

Yet in the chasm of his flesh

An old fire born of a tree

Calmly burns on

Das Kohlejahr

Aus meinem Kohlejahr

Schält sich mein Vogelaug

Ganz angepaßt der Rundung einer Nacht

Und blickt und blickt

Ins Herz des Zinns in die Glut des Orion

Kohle mein Trauerhaupt

Steig aus dem Wald des Alterns und des Werdens

Es öffnet sich die Schläfe von Gestein

Im Gletscher eines Diamants

Erglühn die sieben Prismen meines Bluts

Year of Coal

In my year of coal

My bird's eye is peeled

And aligned with the curve of night

It gazes and gazes

Into the tin heart in the embers of Orion

O coal, my head of mourning

Rise from the forest of aging and becoming

My temples are released from the rock

The seven prisms of my blood

Glow in the glacier of a diamond

Rosentum

Mondrose

Die in Tierköpfen brennt

Hirnrose

Aus Schädeln geschält

O jähes Rosentum

Solang das Rad der Rose

Schwingt und schwingt

Die Mittagsroserei

In Äckern fiebert

Bohrt sich das Rosenaug

In meinen wachen Schlaf

Doch wehe wenn die Unrose

Aus den Metallen steigt

Und meine Rosenhand sich hebt

Gegen die Sonnenrose

Und die Sandrose welkt

O Rose Rose der Rosen

Die nur dem Rosenlosen loht

Rosedom

Moon-rose

That burns in the heads of beasts

Brain-rose

Skinned from skulls

O hot-tempered rosedom

As long as the wheel of the rose

Turns and turns

The noonday rosary

Raves in fevered fields

And the rose-eye bores

Into my waking sleep

Yet woe if the Unrose

Ascends from the metals

And my rose-hand rises

Against the sun-rose

And the sand-rose withers

O rose rose of roses

That alone blazes for the roseless

Erde

Wirf dich an die Erde

Hör den Pferdehuf im Herzen

Klopfe an die Erde

Blutangst springt dir ins Gehirn

Grab die Erde

Trüffelfäulnis zeigt dir ihr Geschlecht

Küß die Erde

Und Gewürm füllt Hände dir und Mund

Earth

Hurl yourself on the earth

Hear the horse hoof in your heart

Beat on the earth

Fear of blood bursts into your brain

Dig in the earth

Truffle rot shows you its sex

Kiss the earth

And vermin fill your hands and mouth

Hiob

I

Mondaxt

Sink in mein Mark

Daß meine Zeder

Morgen den Weg versperre

Den feurigen Pferden

Alte Löwen meines Bluts

Rufen umsonst nach Gazellen

Es morschen in meinem Kopf

Wurmstichige Knochen

Phosphoreszent

Hängt mir im Brustkorb

Das fremde Herz

Job

I

Moon axe

Sink into my marrow

So that tomorrow my cedar

Blocks the path

Of the flaming horses

Old lions in my blood

Call in vain for gazelles

Wormy bones

Rot in my head

An alien heart

Hangs phosphorescent

In my ribcage

II

Verzehre mich, greiser Kalk

Zerlauge mich, junges Salz

Tod ist Freude

Und nährt mich noch der Fisch

Des Toten Meeres

Leuchtend von Jod

In meinen Geschwüren

Pfleg ich die Rosen

Des Todesfrühlings

Siebzig Scheunen verbrannt!

Sieben Söhne verwest!

Größe der Armut!

Letzter Ölbaum

Aus Asiens Wüste

Steht mein Gerippe

Wieso ich noch lebe?

Unsicherer Gott

Dich dir zu beweisen

II

Devour me, hoary lime

Leach me, young salt

Death is joy

And that fish in the Dead Sea

Lit up with iodine

Still feeds me

In my boils

I cultivate the roses

Of death's spring

Seventy barns burned!

Seven sons destroyed!

The largesse of poverty!

The last olive tree

From Asia's desert

Is my skeleton

Why am I still alive?

To prove you to yourself

O insecure God!

III

Letzter Ölbaum, sagst du?

Doch goldenes Öl

Enttrieft meinen Zweigen

Die segnen lernten

Im Glashaus meiner Augen

Reift die tropische Sonne

Mein Wurzelfuß ist in Marmor gerammt

Höre Israel

Ich bin der Zehnbrotebaum

Ich bin das Feuerbuch

Mit den brennenden Buchstaben

Ich bin der dreiarmige Leuchter

Von wissenden Vögeln bewohnt

Mit dem siebenfarbenen Blick

III

Last olive tree, you say?

Yet golden oil

Drips from my branches

That learned how to bless

In the glass house of my eyes

The tropical sun grows hot

My root-foot is rammed in marble

Hear O Israel

I am the ten-bread tree

I am the book of fire

With the burning letters

I am the three-armed chandelier

Occupied by knowing birds

With their seven-colored gaze

Süd

Südwind rüttelt an meinen Wirbeln

Eine Tür in meiner Brust springt auf

Aber welche ist's von allen Türen

Sag welche ist's durch die ich mir entflieh?

Süd brüderlicher Süd

Wisch weg von meiner Stirn die Frage

Schmelze den Einsamen los

Aus den schmerzenden Gletschern

South

The South Wind rattles in my vertebrae

A door in my chest bursts open

But of all the doors which one is it?

Tell me which it is so I can flee from myself

South brotherly South

Brush the question from my brow

Thaw this loner free

From the grieving glaciers

Ozeanlied

Schwesternwelle im grünen Haar

Salzwelle die nie sich versäult und versäumt

Daß von euch Tausenden nur eine

Den Schicksalsarm um mich rundete

Nur eine das Haupt mir tragen hülfe

Und wir zusammen niedertaumelten

Die todlose Treppe

Des Zeit-Ozeans

Dem Pole des Gehorsams zu

Ocean Song

Sister wave with the green hair

Salt wave that never hardened and lingered

Of all you thousands of waves only one

Put her fateful arm around me

Only one would help me hold up my head

And we tumbled down together

Down the deathless steps

Of the ocean of time

To the Pole of Obedience

Schnee-Masken

Es hat der Schnee über Nacht

Meine Totenmaske gemacht

Weiß war das Lachen des Schnees

Und meinen Schatten verwandelt

Er in ein Fastnachtsgewand

Ein Sturm von goldnen Triangeln

Hat plötzlich die tönende Stadt

Gehoben aus all ihren Angeln

Im tausendjährigen Licht

Wurden die Türme der Zeit

Von ihren Ankern befreit

Der Schnee hat über Nacht

Mein Traumgesicht wahrgemacht

Snow Masks

Overnight the snow

Made my death mask

White was the snow's laughter

And it turned my shadow

Into a carnival costume

Suddenly a storm of golden triangles

Raised the ringing city

Off all its hinges

In thousand-year-old light

The towers of time

Were set free from their anchors

Overnight the snow

Made my dream face come true

In den Äckern des Kampfers

In den Äckern des Kampfers bist du daheim

In den Sümpfen des Jods trinkst du dich endlich jung

Die braunen Schnäpse der Wurzeln

Nähren dich besser als die Krüge der Sonne

Eine Fackel loht und torkelt im Öl deiner Augen

Ein Feuer musiziert mit Flöte und Tamtam:

Gebein der Ahnen tanzt zum Fest der Verwesung

Die gelbe adelige Blume

Die alle tausend Jahre einmal blüht

Windet sich langsam aus deinem Brustkorb

In Fields of Camphor

You are at home in fields of camphor

In iodine swamps you drink yourself finally young

The brown brandy of roots

Nourishes you better than jugs of sun

A torch blazes and reels in the oil of your eyes

A fire makes music with flute and drum

Your ancestors' skeleton dances at the festival of decay

The noble yellow flower

That blooms once every thousand years

Slowly uncoils from your ribcage

Die Sonnen-Kantate

Es tanzt der vielarmige Gott für uns
Es denkt das feuerhaarige Haupt und singt
Lichtpauke tönt und Meeresharfe
Ihn zu begrüßen den Wunderbaren

Von welchem Feuerbaume bist du gerollt
O Frucht die ihren eigenen Kern verzehrt
Und die ich brennend noch vom Phosphor
In die unwissenden Hände nehme

Die Nuß in deren Schale der Ursinn wohnt
Die nackte Nuß vom eigenen Genuß betört
Sich immer wieder selbst gebärend
Irres Gesetz ihrer Selbstanbetung

Noch ungeborne Sonnen des Kohleschachts
Und schon verbrauchte Sonnen des Abendrauchs
Bouquets von blauen Sonnen bind ich
Nächte euch blinderen unaufhörlich

The Sun Cantata

The many-armed god dances for us

The fire-haired chieftain ponders and sings

    Light-drum and sea-harp resound

    To greet Him the Wondrous One

From which tree of fire did you fall

O fruit that consumes its own seed

    That still burning of phosphorus

    I take in my unwitting hands

The nut in whose shell the primal mind lives

The naked nut beguiled by its own pleasure

    Begets itself over and over

    In the crazed law of self adoration

Yet unborn suns of coalmines

And already consumed suns of evening smoke

    I bind in bouquets of blue suns

    For your incessant blind nights

Den Mittag sägt das Zahnrad der Ungeduld

Der Sonnenblume stehender Schlaf erschlafft

Uns fallen Mandeln aus den Augen

Pfirsiche springen wie Meteore

O Sonne! Werde grausam mit deinem Korn!

Leg deine Todeseier in unser Ohr!

Auf daß aus jeder Schädelspalte

Kupfern die Blume des Wahnsinns blühe!

Im Sonnenkopfe altert die gelbe Zeit

Die Zeit die sich verdenkt und vergißt! Die Zeit

Des Sturzbachs und des faulen Teiches

Fallender Monde in blinden Himmeln

Eisvogel Zeit im Sonnengedächtnis! Sing

Die ungeliebten Frühlinge: Sing das Herz

Das seit Jahrtausenden verschüttet

Aus den Rubinen des Bergs dich anruft!

The cogwheel of impatience saws away the noon

The sunflower grows weary in its standing sleep

    Almonds fall from our eyes

    Peaches plunge like meteors

O Sun! Be cruel with your seed!

Lay your death eggs in our ear!

    So that from each cranial crack

    The flower of madness blooms copper!

In the sun's head amber time grows old

Time that loses itself in thought and forgets! Time

    Of the plunging brook and the putrid pond

    Of falling moons in blind skies

Ice-bird time in the sun's memory! Sing

Of the uncherished springtimes: Sing of the heart

    Which buried alive for millennia

    Calls you from the rubies in the mountain!

Drei Oden an Claire

I

Tief hängt die Regenwolke in deinen Traum

Die Früchte der Verheißung sind überreif

Im Spinnweb deines Angesichts

Faulen die Sterne der Auferstehung

Daß auch der Venus heiliges Haupt im Gras

Vermoosen soll, das ähnlichste dir, und schon

Vom herbstlichen Gefühl bereift

Blinder Vergessenheit karge Wohnung

Ich halte deinen Kopf mit der Eierstirn

Durch die dein Hirn im Phosphorgespräch mir scheint

Wie eine fleischfressende Rose

Rollest, o rollest du mir von dannen

Three Odes to Claire

I

The rain cloud hangs low in your reverie

Fruits of promise are overripe

Stars of the resurrection rot

In the cobweb of your countenance

That even the holy head of Venus,

The most like you, should gather moss

In the grass already frosty with autumn

Meager dwelling of blind oblivion

I hold your head with its egg-shaped brow

Through which your brain glows in phosphorescent talk

Like a flesh-eating rose

You roll, o you roll away from me

II

Leg an mein Ohr dein silbernes Muschelohr

Und sag kein Wort: ich höre was du verschweigst

Und was du selber nie geahnt hast

Rollende Brandung der Leidenschaften

Es klingt aus dir der manische Ozean

Es ruft aus dir der Gott mit dem dunklen Mund

Der voller Drohung ist und Anklag

Wenn eine rote Geige aufschluchzt in deinem Fest

Bild ich mir ein, ich führte den Bogen

Jedoch von selber schwingt dein Körper

Nicht ich war der Künstler, nicht ich

II

Move your silver-mussel ear next to mine

And don't say a word: I can hear your secrets

And what you yourself have never sensed

The rolling surf of your passions

From your depths the manic ocean resounds

From you the God with the dark mouth calls

Full of menace and accusation

When a red violin sobs at your fête

I imagine I am guiding the bow

Yet your body swings on its own

I was not the artist, not I

III

In deinem Aug sind unsre Paläste schon

Vom Salz verzehrt, ist bröckelndes Leuchtergold

Von alten Fischen angefressen:

Unerkannt steh ich vor seinen Ufern!

Und seh dich im smaragdenen Geisterschiff

Verführt vom eigenwilligen Jupiter

Mir ohne Warnung weggetragen

Dieweil dein Mund voller Sehnsucht tönet

Von deinen innern Spiegeln schon ganz betört

Wie tausendfach durchschauertes Bergkristall

Hat sich dein Wahrsein ganz entkleidet:

Deine opalene Seele strahlt mir!

III

In your eye our palaces have already

Been consumed by salt, old fishes

Have gnawed at the crumbling candelabra gold:

Unrecognized I stand on its shores!

I watch you in a phantom ship of emeralds

Seduced by mighty Jupiter

Borne away from me without warning

All the while your lips cry out in longing

Already bewitched by your inner mirrors

Like rock crystal shot with a thousand tremors

Your true being is stripped bare:

Your opalescent soul shines upon me!

An Claire-Liliane

Geliebte du mein Strom

An deinem rechten Ufer steht das Vergangene

An deinem linken Ufer steht das Werdende

Zusammenströmend singen wir die Gegenwart

Sie sehen uns nach, die Bäume der Verwesung

Sie fliegen uns voraus, die Vögel der Erlösung

In deinem rechten Auge bin ich Diamant

In meinem linken Auge bist du Samt

Die Sonne rollt von deiner rechten Schulter

Der Mond verwest in meiner linken Hand

Geliebte ich dein Strom

Zusammenfließend schweigen wir die Gegenwart

To Claire-Liliane

Beloved, you are my river

On your right bank is the past

On your left bank is the future

Streaming together we sing the present

The decaying trees, they gaze after us

The birds of deliverance, they fly before us

In your right eye I am a diamond

In my left eye you are velvet

The sun revolves from your right shoulder

The moon wanes in my left hand

Beloved, I am your river

Flowing together we are silent in the present

Ψ

Dein Kopf aus Knochen aus Wolken aus Feuer

Ich nehm ihn oft in meine schweren Hände

Ich kann ihn schütteln, ich kann ihn drehen.

Ich höre drinnen Wasserfälle stürzen, Welten gären

O mein erhabener Kopf!

Diese Saphirsterne! Auf- und untergehend!

Wie quäl ich diesen Kopf! Ich fülle ihn mit Tränen!

Ich laß ihn wehrlos altern!

Und denke nie: hier drinnen waltet Gott!

ψ

Your head of bones of clouds of fire

I take it often in my heavy hands

I can shake it, I can turn it

Inside I hear waterfalls tumble, worlds in ferment

O my sublime head!

These sapphire stars! Rising and setting!

How I torment this head! I fill it with tears!

I let it grow old unprotected!

And never think: here inside reigns God!

Ψ

Deine linke Hand ist eine Blumendolde

Deine rechte eine Knochenblume!

Beide segnen mich, beide nähren mich

Mit dem Blut der Vögel, mit dem Fleisch der Götter.

Deine Hände lächeln, trauern, schwirren,

Steigen auf und ab wie Schalen einer Waage

Und kaum wende ich den Blick von einer zur andern

Bin ich schon ein Greis geworden

ψ

Your left hand is a flower umbel

Your right a flower of bones!

Both bless me, both nurture me

With the blood of birds, with the flesh of gods.

Your hands smile, mourn, flit about,

Move up and down like the trays of a scale

And barely do I glance from one to the other

Than I have become an old man

Ψ

Belauscher deines Schlafs

Hör ich die blinde Pianistin

Auf deinen Rippen spielen

Hör ich die schwarzen Wellen der Nacht

An deiner zarten Brüstung branden

Das Tier der Angst durch deine Büsche stampfen

Und Brücken über deinen Blutstrom bersten

Belauscher deines Schlafs

Zähl ich die Pulse meiner Zeit

ψ

Eavesdropping on your sleep

I hear the blind pianist

Playing on your ribs

I hear the black waves of night

Breaking on your tender breastwork

The brute angst stomping through your bushes

And bridges bursting over your bloodstream

Eavesdropping on your sleep

I count the pulse of my days

ψ

Du mit den Zeisigaugen, mit den Veilchenaugen

Wie soll ich nur deine Gedanken deuten?

Aus deinem Munde spricht die Quelle

Durch deine Adern wandert

Dein uferloses Volk

Es schmausen Könige an deiner Tafel

Und ihre Weisheit macht dich blaß und blasser

Aber die rosa Mandelbäumchen

Sie wachsen aus dem Herzen dir

Und deine Lerchen- deine Himbeeraugen zwitschern

ψ

You with the siskin eyes, with the eyes of violets

How should I interpret just your thoughts?

From your mouth the source speaks

Through your veins wander

Boundless throngs of your people

Kings feast at your table

And their wisdom makes you paler and paler

But pink almond trees

Grow from your heart

And larks chirp in your raspberry eyes

ψ

Liebender zu sein, ach, wer erfaßt es

Klarer als mit erblindetem Aug!

Liebender zu sein und aller Entscheidung

Beraubt und allen Gerichten

Längst entrückt!

Die sinnlose Herrschaft der Berge

Ist abgeschafft und auch des Enzians

Treuloses Blau. Die Sonne geht irr

Es wütet umsonst die kinderlose Mitternacht.

Denn Liebender zu sein

Und wissender Bote

Ist höchster Adel

ψ

To be a lover, ah, who grasps it

More clearly than with a blind eye!

To be a lover and

Robbed of all decision

And long since removed from all courts of law!

The senseless rule of the mountains

And the fickle blue of the gentian

Have been abolished. The sun goes awry

Childless midnight rages in vain.

For to be a lover

And a wise messenger

Is the highest nobility

ψ

Wieviele Morgensonnen haben ihr Ebenbild

In unserem Vieraug erschaut!

Und des Tages Gestaltung stand unsrer Willkür anheim.

ı

Der reinen Erfindung der Liebe

Verdankte der Tau seine Dauer

Und wo Taifune an Urwaldgetier sich mästeten

Und ihre langen gelben Flügel

Um schwankende Inseln warfen

Selbst da hielt unser lebend Liebesdenkmal stand

Löste dein Lächeln Geliebte

Die dunkelsten Rätsel auf

ψ

How many morning suns have seen

Their image reflected in our eyes!

And the shaping of the day was at our discretion

The dew owed its existence

To the pure invention of love

Even where typhoons grew fat on jungle beasts

And threw their long yellow wings

Around unstable islands

Even there our living monument to love stood firm

Your smile, my beloved,

Solved the darkest riddles of all

ψ

Mit Atem besiegte ich dich: Du Ahnungslose

Mit Atem trieb ich die Halme deines Roggenhaars hoch

Mit Atem blies ich aufs Feuer deiner Ängste

Du glaubtest noch an die Macht des Sturms

Und nicht an die Macht des Manns

Mit meinem Atem vertrieb ich die Engel

Die dich heimsuchten

In der Wolke meines abendlichen Atems

Trieben wir von allen Ufern fort

ψ

With my breath I conquered you when least suspecting

With my breath I made the stalks of your rye hair stand on end

With my breath I fanned the fire of your fears

Back then you still believed in the power of the storm

But not in the power of the man

With my breath I banished the angels

That plagued you

In the cloud of my evening breath

We drifted away from all shores

Ψ

Ich höre steigen aus dir den frierenden Vogel des Morgens,

Den heiseren, aus den gütigen Öfen des Schlafes

Geliebte, mein Feuer!

Ich höre fallen aus dir die dunkle Sprache des Mittags,

Den ernsten, gereiften Granat der langen weiseren Duldung,

Erde, meine Geliebte!

I höre rufen in dir das goldene Tierhorn des Abends,

Die tiefbegründete Angst vor der ungewissen Vollendung,

Meine Geliebte, die Luft!

Ich höre rauschen durch dich die alten Meere der Mitternacht

Und drohende Magie des nimmer erlahmenden Atems,

Wasser, meine Geliebte!

ψ

I hear the freezing bird of morning take flight from you,

The raucous one, from the benevolent ovens of sleep

Beloved, my fire!

I hear the dark language of noon tumble out of you,

The stern, mature garnet of long wise tolerance

Earth, my beloved!

I hear the golden ram's horn of evening call in you,

The deeply buried fear of an uncertain end,

My beloved, the air!

I hear the old seas of midnight rush through you

And the menacing magic of never-wearying breath,

Water, my beloved!

Die Himmelfahrt

Wie die Lerche stürzte ich kopfüber

In die Kuppeln deiner Augen

Um im Azur mein Ur zu finden

Ich sang um dich zu entführen

Aus dem Halbschlaf der Ahnen und Toten

Unsterblich wandeltest du

An Schloßruinen des Mondes entlang

Und meine dunkle Harfe erreichte dich nicht

Unmerklich drehte sich dein Kopf gen Osten

Nie fand ich den Weg zurück zu heimischen Gärten

The Ascension

Like the lark I fell head over heels

Into the domes of your eyes

Seeking in their azure my source

I sang intending to kidnap you

From the half-sleep of ancestors and the dead

Immortal, you strolled alongside

Castle ruins of the moon

And my dark harp did not reach you

Imperceptibly your head turned toward the East

I have never found the way back to my native gardens

An Claire

Geschrieben im Spital des Todes,
Dezember 1949 bis Januar 1950

Hab ich dich gepflückt in den Gärten von Ephesus

Das krause Haar deiner Nelken

Den Abendstrauß der Hände?

Hab ich dich gefischt in den Seen des Traums

Ich warf dir mein Herz zur Speisung

Ein Angler an deinen Weidenufern

Hab ich dich gefunden in der Dürre der Wüste

Du warst mein letzter Baum

Du warst die letzte Frucht meiner Seele

Von deinem Schlaf nun umfangen bin ich

In deine Ruhe tief gebettet

Wie der Mandelkern in nachtbraune Schale

To Claire

Written in the Hospice
December 1949 to January 1950

Did I pluck you in the gardens of Ephesus

The curly hair of your carnations

The evening bouquet of your hands?

Did I fish for you in the lakes of dream?

An angler on your meadows' shores

I threw you my heart for food

Did I find you in the dryness of the desert?

You were my last tree

You were the last fruit of my soul

Now I am wrapped in your sleep

Bedded deep in your repose

Like the almond in its night-brown shell

ψ

Es spricht sich die Sage herum

Daß deine Füße zum Fischschwanz werden

Wenn du nach Meerfrüchten für mich tauchst

Die Kinder flüstern schon

Daß deine Arme Weidenzweige sind

In denen sich die Wolken verfangen

In die du mich bettest

Es ist kein Geheimnis mehr

Daß deine Lippen bluten

Um mich in den Nächten des Sterbens

Vom schneeigen Hunger zu retten

Bald wird man wissen daß dein Körper gehöhlt ist

Ein duftendes Grab

Für unseren Zwillingstod

ψ

The rumor is spreading

That your feet become a fish tail

When you dive to fetch me fruit from the sea

The children are already whispering

That your arms are willow branches

That catch the clouds

Where you bed me down

It is no longer a secret

That your lips bleed

To save me from snowy hunger

In my nights of dying

Soon everyone will know

That your body has been hollowed

A fragrant grave

For our twin death

Ψ

Aus meinen Knochen trinke das Kiefernmark

Aus meinen Augen schlage die Austernperle

Belege mit Perlmutterplatten

Unsrer Erinnerung Traumschiff

Im Gottesacker blüht meine Asterhand

Der Staubgefäße reifende Liebesschrift

Verstreue ihre Samenkörner

Säe im Nachtraum dein neues Sternbild

Im Diadem der mondenen Zauberin

Dreizehntes Bild des rasenden Zodiaks

Erstrahlt die Blume des Totenfeldes

Glühende Lilie meines Herzens

ψ

Drink the marrow of my jawbone

Beat the oyster's pearl from my eyes

Cover the dreamboat of our memory

With panels of mother-of-pearl

In the churchyard my aster hand blooms

As the ripening love-script of stamens

Scatter their grains of pollen

Sow your new constellation in night's expanse

In the diadem of the sorceress of the moon

The flower in the graveyard gleams

Thirteenth sign of the raging zodiac

Glowing lily of my heart

Ψ

In deinem Haupte streichle ich das Feuer das mich sengt

In deiner zauberischen Stirneninschrift

Entziffere ich die Rätsel meiner Einsamkeit

In den verhaltenen Fluten deiner Aquamarine

Nahm ich ein hundertjährig Bad der Tiefe

Und verlor mein eigenes Schwergewicht

Geliebte wenn wir einmal untergehen

Zerfallen die Ruinen unsres seligen Turms und unsre Engel

Verlieren die Flügel beim Sturz in den Abgrund

ψ

In your head I caress the fire that singes me

In the bewitching inscription on your brow

I decipher the riddles of my loneliness

In the stemmed tide of your aquamarine eyes

I took a deep hundred-year bath

And lost my own gravity

Beloved, when we one day perish

The ruins of our hallowed tower will collapse

And our angels will lose their wings plunging into the abyss

ψ

Aus Gräbern steigt aus Schattengenist das Ei

Der Vogelsonne nach der verstaubten Nacht

Und deine diamantene Stimme

Wirft sich im Flugsturz um meine Seele

Aus unsrem zwiegewundenen Rosenstock

Der schwarzen Winterwinde noch kaum entkeimt

Erstrahlt die einmalige Rose

Unserer Körper erlauchter Blutkuß

Erlöse uns, orangener Tagplanet!

Uns zu erkennen haben drei Augen wir

Wie jene Götter fremder Tempel

Denen die Liebe Vollendung brachte

ψ

Out of the shadow-nest of graves

The bird-sun egg climbs after the dusty night

And your diamond voice flings itself

In flight-fall around my soul

From our intertwined rose vine

Barely sprouted in the black winter winds

The solitary rose glows

Noble blood-kiss of our bodies

Redeem us, orange day planet!

We are known by our three eyes

Like those gods of foreign temples

To whom love brought perfection

ψ

Deine Trauerampel Geliebte

Scheint durch alle Fernen zu mir

Wie die geröteten Augen

Der tiefergriffenen Sterne

Ich trank die Becher entscheidender Weine

Während ich einsam war

Und deinem Weinberg entrückt

Wie kommt's daß die Sonne goldner rauscht

Wenn ich die Augen schließe

Und daß dein Blut gewaltiger in mir pulst

Wenn du Entrissene

Nur noch mit Nebelarmen mich mahnst?

ψ

Beloved, your hanging lamp of mourning

Beams to me through outer space

Like the reddened eyes

Of deeply anguished stars

While I was lonely

And entranced by your vineyard

I drank wines that proved crucial

How is it that the sun glitters more golden

When I close my eyes

And your blood pulses in me more strongly

When you who have been wrenched away

Warn me with nothing but arms of mist?

ψ

Wer immer dir begegnet, merke den Ernst der Nächte

Die mit wilden Flügeln bewaffnet

Das leere Heim der Einsamen heimsuchen

Merke, daß du liebst und blutest

Schwankend vergehst wie die Kelche

Der Rosen am Marterweg

Daß von deiner Schulter entströmt das Unträumbare

Das Unsinnbare eines großen Wissens

Und was auch immer die Engel vermögen

Sie spenden die Ruhe solcher Erfahrung nicht

Du bist das Sternbild das immer wieder sich bildet

Du bist das Löwenfell in das sich die Sonne kleidet

Betraure zu tief nicht den Totenfalter

Laß die frostbedrohten Pfirsiche meiner Träume

In deinem Sommeratem weiterreifen

ψ

Whoever crosses your path, note the solemnity of the nights

That armed with wild wings

Haunt the barren dwelling of the lonely

Note that you love and bleed

Trembling, you disappear like the chalices

Of roses on the martyrs' path

Note the undreamable streaming from your shoulder

The unthinkable of great knowledge

And whatever else the angels can do

They do not grant the repose of such worldly wisdom

You are the constellation that fashions itself ever new

You are the lion skin that clothes the sun

Do not mourn the death moth too deeply

Let the frost-threatened peaches of my dreams

Further ripen in your summer breath

ψ

Ich war der Fragende und du die Magierin

Auf dem Dreistuhl der Zeit

Ich brachte dir mein Traumtier zum Opfer

Du gabst mir zurück den Rauch der Erinnerung

Es war ein Hirsch geritzt in deine Stirn

Aus deinen grünen Schluchten vernahm ich

Den niegehörten Gesang

Wozu drang ich hinab in deine Feuerberge?

Ich habe längst vergessen, was ich heischte:

Die Liebe oder die Erkenntnis

ψ

I was the seeker and you the sorceress

On the three-legged stool of time

I brought you my totem as sacrifice

In return you gave me the smoke of memory

It was a stag etched into your forehead

From your green glens I perceived

A song never heard before

Why did I descend into your volcanoes?

I have long since forgotten what I was seeking

Was it love or understanding?

ψ

Fremd ist mir meines Haupthaars rostige Wolle

Und feindlich fast des Muskels Gehorsam im Arm

Doch wie bekannt und hingegeben

Die Wendung deines nahen Halses

Mir zugehörig auch

Der Pfeil der Zugvögel

In deinem wolkigen Aug

Wie zielbewußt in meine berstende Stirn gesendet

Mich meines wogenden Blutes beraubend

Wie meinen Händen eingefühlt

Die zarte Neigung deines Rückgrats

Deine kaum sichtbaren Flügel

Gefügt aus den Schwingen zerbrochener Vögel

Und dein Körper geknetet aus Schnee

ψ

Foreign is the rusty wool of the hair on my head

And almost hostile the obedience of the muscle in my arm

Yet how familiar and devoted

The way you turn your head toward me!

Mine too is the dart

Of migrating birds

In your cloudy eye

How purposefully shot into my bursting forehead

Robbing me of my surging blood!

How my hands are filled to overflowing!

The tender incline of your spine

Your barely visible wings

Wrought from the pinions of broken birds

And your body kneaded out of snow

Die Angst-Tänzerin

Die Angst deiner Hände ist leicht wie der Rauch über Äckern

Du bist gefangen im Dornturm

Du schwebst durch die Mauern hindurch und gelangst doch nimmer
    zu mir

Die Angst deiner Haare ist gelb wie der Schein vergehender Kerzen

Die Angst deiner Stimme ist undurchdringlich wie Nebel

Du wirfst dich an meine Brust und dennoch spür ich dich nicht

Du bist eine Angst-Tänzerin als Herbstzeitlose verkleidet

Im Kreise von roten Kriegern beschwingt dich Knochenmusik

Doch nimmer sprengst du den Kreis und nimmer schwebst du zu mir

Was flüstert in deinem Kopf? Wen nennst du deinen Bedränger?

Nie schwelte so trügerisch das rötliche Grün deiner Augen

Als im Gespräch mit dem waffenglitzernden Feind

Die Angst ist das glühende Wollkleid das blaue das ich dir gekauft

Es umfängt dich und läßt dich nicht her bis zu mir

Du brennst in seinem Geweb und dein Ruf ist ein klagender Vogel

The Fear Dancer

The fear in your hands is light as smoke over fields

You are caught in a tower of thorns

You glide through its walls yet you never find your way to me

The fear in your hair is yellow as the glow of dying candles

The fear in your voice is inscrutable as fog

You hurl yourself against my chest and yet I cannot feel you

You are a fear dancer disguised as autumn crocus

In a circle of red warriors you are buoyed by the music of bones

Yet you never break the circle and you never glide to me

What is whispering in your head? Whom do you call your tormentor?

Never has the reddish-green of your eyes smoldered so deceitfully

As in your dealings with the weapon-glistening foe

Fear is the burning wool dress--the blue one that I bought for you

It embraces you and keeps you from coming to me

You are burning in its fabric and crying like a wailing bird

Der Regenpalast

Ich hab dir einen Regenpalast erbaut

Aus Alabastersäulen und Bergkristall

Daß du in tausend Spiegeln

Immer schöner dich für mich wandelst

Die Wasserpalme nährt uns mit grauem Most

Aus hohen Krügen trinken wir silbernen Wein

Welch ein perlmutternes Konzert!

Trunkne Libelle im Regenurwald!

Im Käfig der Lianen ersehnst du mich

Die Zauberbienen saugen das Regenblut

Aus deinen blauen Augenkelchen

Singende Reiher sind deine Wächter

Aus Regenfenstern blicken wir wie die Zeit

Mit Regenfahnen über das Meer hinweht

Und mit dem Schlachtheer fremder Stürme

Elend in alten Morästen endet

The Rain Palace

I have built you a rain palace

Of alabaster columns and rock crystal

    So you can transform yourself for me

    Ever more beautiful in a thousand mirrors

The water palm nourishes us with its gray grog

We drink silver wine from tall pitchers

    What mother-of-pearl drumming!

    Drunken dragonfly in the rain forest!

In your liana cage of vines you long for me

Magic bees suck the rain-blood

    From your blue-eyed goblets

    Singing herons stand guard

From rain-windows we watch how time

Drifts with rain-banners across the sea

    And with battle troops of foreign storms

    Ends miserably in ancient swamps

Mit Regendiamanten bekleid ich dich

Heimlicher Maharadscha des Regenreichs

Des Wert und Recht gewogen wird

Nach den gesegneten Regenjahren

Du aber strickst mir verstohlen im Perlensaal

Durchwirkt von Hanf und Träne ein Regentuch

Ein Leichentuch breit für uns beide

Bis in die Ewigkeit warm und haltbar

I dress you in rain-diamonds

Disguised Maharaja of the Realm of Rain

    Whose worth and laws are weighed

    In hallowed years of rain

But on the sly in the Hall of Pearls you knit me

A rain-shawl from hemp and tears

    Wide enough for us both

    A warm and everlasting shroud

Das Wüstenhaupt

Ich baute mir dein Haupt über der Wüste des täglichen Todes

Zahllose Sklaven brannten die Ziegel deiner Gestalt

Aus dem Blut des Sonnenaufgangs

Auf Regenleitern stiegen Maurer in deine Augen

Legten die Kuppeln aus mit dem Goldstaub der Sterne

Und die Pupillen mit Kohol und Smaragd

Diese schwebten wie die ewige Waage

Auf der sich Sonne und Mond messen

Bald stieg aus dem Tor deines granitenen Mundes

Der wahr-und irrsprach

Die Zauberlehre deines alten Volkes

Ich glaubte dein Herz für immer geborgen

In der tiefsten Wohnung der Wüste

Dein Seherinnenauge die Zeit überstrahlend

Doch ach wie bald erblindetest du

Im Sandwind und Nebel der Geister

Die Ziegel verwesten schneller als alles Fleisch

Die Karawanen die am Salzsee deiner Augen lagerten

The Desert Head

Above the desert of daily death I built myself your head

Countless slaves baked bricks of your form

From the blood of the rising sun

Masons climbed on rain-ladders into your eyes

Covering their domes with the gold dust of stars

And their pupils with kohl and emerald

These swayed like the eternal scales

On which the sun and moon compete

Then from the gate of your granite mouth

Prophecies spewed forth both true and false

Magic teachings of your ancient people

I believed your heart was safe forever

In the deepest dwelling of the desert

Your seer's eye shining through the ages

Yet oh how soon you were blinded

In the sandstorm and fog of ghosts

The bricks decayed more quickly than all flesh

Caravans that camped at the salt lake of your eyes

Erkannten dein verwehendes Haupt nicht mehr

Und deiner bröckelnden Lippen Gesang

Verschallte im blauen Gewölbe des Mondes

No longer recognized your weatherworn head

And the song on your crumbling lips

Died away in the blue vault of the moon

Tochter der Tiefe

Du Tochter der Tiefe, wie halt ich dich im Glashaus des Mondes

Wie verbind ich dein magisches Aug mit den Wolken des schnellen
    Vergessens

Wie gewöhn ich dich an die Rundheit der Erde?

Vom Neumond Besessene

Wie bändige ich dein Binnenmeer

Das über die Ufer des Menschlichen wogt?

Wie fang ich die Feuerfische in meinen ungläubigen Netzen?

Und wenn der Vollmond dich schwängert mit Samen des Mohns

Wie kühl ich das Fieber der schlaflosen Berge

Wie blend ich ab die Todesstrahlen deiner Rubine?

Ach nur im abnehmenden Mond

Da magern die Flüsse ab und erlischt

Das Ginster-Irrlicht deiner Augen

Dein rauher Ruf wie der der heiligen Tiere

Ergibt sich meinem jagenden Herzen

Daughter of the Deep

Daughter of the deep, how do I hold you in the glass house of the
    moon?

How do I link your magical eye to the clouds of swift forgetting?

How do I accustom you to the roundness of the earth?

Possessed as you are by the new moon

How do I tame your inland sea

That surges over the shores of humanity?

How do I catch the lionfish in my infidel nets?

And when the full moon sows you with the poppy's seeds

How do I cool the fever of the sleepless mountains?

How do I dim the death beams of your rubies?

Only under the waning moon

Do the rivers ebb and the lights die

In the will-'o-the-wisp of your eyes

Your harsh call like that of the holy beasts

Surrenders to my racing heart

Die Aschenhütte

Wir hatten kein Haus wie die andern an sicherem Berghang

Wir mußten immer weiterwandern

Im Schnee der weder Salz noch Zucker war

An runden Kegeln des Mondes entlang

Du riefst nach deinen Schutzvögeln

Die hoch im Äther zu den Gräbern Afrikas flogen

Die Straße des Vergessens machte große Schleifen

Und keine blasse Blume sann am Weg

Gen Mitternacht fand sich eine Aschenhütte

Man hörte das lachende Bellen der Wölfe

Mit Fackeln hielt ich sie fern

Und fing im Nesselbach einen Ölfisch

Der uns lange erwärmte

Breit war das Bett aus geschnitztem Schnee

Und da geschah das Wunder:

Dein goldener Leib erstrahlte als nächtliche Sonne

The Ash Hut

We had no house like the others on a safe mountain slope

We always had to keep wandering

In the snow that was neither salt nor sugar

Along the round ten-pins of the moon

You called to your guardian birds

That flew high in the ether to the graves of Africa

The road of forgetting made great loops

And no pale flower brooded by the wayside

Around midnight an ash hut appeared

You could hear the laughing bark of the wolves

With torches I held them at bay

And caught an oilfish in the thistle creek

That warmed us through the night

Broad was our bed carved from snow

And then the miracle happened:

Your golden body shone like the night sun

Der Salzsee

Der Mond leckt wie ein Wintertier das Salz deiner Hände,

Doch schäumt dein Haar violett wie ein Fliederbusch,

In dem das erfahrene Käuzchen ruft.

Da steht für uns erbaut die gesuchte Traumstadt,

In der die Straßen alle schwarz und weiß sind.

Du gehst im Glitzerschnee der Verheißung,

Mir sind gelegt die Schienen der dunklen Vernunft.

Die Häuser sind mit Kreide gegen den Himmel gezeichnet

Und ihre Türen bleigegossen;

Nur oben unter Giebeln wachsen gelbe Kerzen

Wie Nägel zu zahllosen Särgen.

Doch bald gelangen wir hinaus zum Salzsee.

Da lauern uns die langgeschnäbelten Eisvögel auf,

Die ich die ganze Nacht mit nackten Händen bekämpfe,

Bevor uns ihre warmen Daunen zum Lager dienen

The Salt Lake

Like a winter animal the moon licks the salt from your hands
Still your hair foams violet as the lilac bush
From where the veteran screech owl calls

There stands our long-sought dream city built just for us
With the streets all black and white
You walk in the glitter-snow of promise
While the rails of dark reason are laid out for me

The houses are drawn with chalk against the sky
And their doors are poured of lead
Only up under the gables yellow candles grow
Like nails for countless coffins

Yet soon we reached the Salt Lake
There the long-billed kingfishers lie in wait
All through the night I fight them with my bare hands
Until their warm down serves as our lair

Der Staubbaum

Ein Staubbaum wächst

Ein Staubwald überall wo wir gegangen

Und diese Staubhand weh! rühr sie nicht an!

Rings um uns steigen Türme des Vergessens

Türme die nach innen fallen

Aber noch bestrahlt von deinem orangenen Licht!

Ein Staubvogel fliegt auf

Die Sage unsrer Liebe laß ich in Quarz verwahren

Das Gold unsrer Träume in einer Wüste vergraben

Der Staubwald wird immer dunkler

Weh! Rühr diese Staubrose nicht an!

The Tree of Dust

A tree of dust is growing

A dust-forest wherever we have gone

And this dust-hand, watch out! Don't touch it!

All around us towers of forgetting are rising

Towers that are caving in

Yet still glow from your orange light!

A dust-bird flies off

I'll have the saga of our love preserved in quartz

The gold of our dreams buried in a desert

The dust-forest is getting darker and darker

Watch out! Don't touch this dust-rose!

Acknowledgments

Grateful acknowledgment is made to the editors of the publications in which these poems first appeared: "Eavesdropping on your Sleep," "I Was the Seeker," and "This Holy Body" in *Asheville Poetry Review*; "The Inner Trees" and "Foreign Is the Rusty Wool" in *International Poetry Review*; "Drink the Marrow of My Jawbone," "Ocean Song," and "Hours" in *House Organ*; "Old Men" and "Rosedom" in *Beloit Poetry Journal*; "The Salt Lake" and "The Blast Furnaces of Pain" in *The Adirondack Review* (online); "Explosion of the Marsh Marigold," "Bloodhound," "Did I pluck you in the gardens of Ephesus," "The Fear-Dancer" in *Shearsman* (UK).

Thanks are due to Wallstein Verlag for permission to use the German text of Yvan Goll's *Traumkraut*; to Robert Johnson for permission to use his painting, "Joe-Pye Weed," on the front cover; to the Fondation Yvan et Claire Goll for permission to use the photograph of Yvan Goll. Special thanks to Dr. Albert Ronsin and his widow, Madame Nadine Ronsin, for their ready willingness to help at every turn. My editor, Diane Goettel, has given clear advice throughout and has been a pleasure to work with.

I'm very grateful to Prof. Helmut Fuhrmann for his interest in this project, for reading the manuscript with great care, and for offering many valuable insights into the translation. Thanks to Galway Kinnell and Robert Bly for sharing their memories of meeting Claire Goll in Paris and for encouraging me in my work. I remember with joy my phone conversations with Miriam Patchen, who graciously recounted her memories of friendship with the Golls and the visits she and her husband Kenneth made to the Golls' townhouse in Brooklyn Heights. Keith Flynn was the first editor to publish any of these translations in his *Asheville Poetry Review*, and I'm grateful that he also celebrated Yvan Goll's poetry in that journal's *Ten Great Neglected Poets of the 20th Century.* My thanks to Jeff Davis for featuring Yvan Goll's poetry on his radio show, "WordPlay," WPVM, Asheville, and to Ralph Buntyn for sharing his insights into Goll's Job poems. I'm pleased that David Meltzer was kind enough to read the manuscript and send along his comments. A tip of my hat to Gerlinde Lindy for relishing my calls for help in untangling the knottiest linguistic snarls.

My unending gratitude goes to Thomas Rain Crowe for introducing me to Yvan Goll's work, for reading and listening critically to my translations, for encouraging and supporting my work always.

About the Author

Yvan Goll, born in Alsace in 1891, mastered both French and German before setting out on his quest for peace and understanding amidst the tumult engulfing his native Europe. He began his journey in Switzerland, flourishing with the Dadaists in Zurich and the pacifists there and in Geneva, then with the German Expressionists in Berlin, the early Surrealists in Paris, across the Atlantic among the artists in Greenwich Village, and finally back to post-war Paris. His oeuvre encompasses poetry, novels, plays, libretti, essays, manifestoes, and translations, often in collaboration with other artists, including James Joyce, Marc Chagall, Kurt Weill, Andre Breton and his wife Claire. When he lived in New York, he also wrote and published in English. Yvan Goll ranks among the great writers of the twentieth century, yet his work is little known to English-speaking audiences. The poems of *Dreamweed* (*Traumkraut*) were conceived in German after he was diagnosed with incurable leukemia. He died in Paris in 1950.

About the Translator

Nan Watkins has degrees in German from Oberlin College and Johns Hopkins University with further study at the University of Munich and the Academy of Music in Vienna. Her translations have appeared in various journals, including *Asheville Poetry Review*, *International Poetry Review*, *Oxygen*, *Beloit Poetry Journal* and *Shearsman* (UK). Her interest in Yvan and Claire Goll led to her essay, "Twin Suns," published in the French catalogue of the 50th anniversary retrospective of Yvan Goll's work, and the translations of Claire Goll's poems in *10,000 Dawns: Love Poems of Yvan & Claire Goll* (White Pine Press, 2004). Her travel memoir, *East Toward Dawn: A Woman's Solo Journey Around the World*, was published by Seal Press in 2002. She lives and works in the Blue Ridge Mountains of North Carolina.